TERE BINA

WITHOUT YOU

DR. YADUVIR SINGH

Copyright © Dr. Yaduvir Singh
All Rights Reserved.

ISBN 978-1-63806-881-5

This book has been published with all efforts taken to make the material error-free after the consent of the author. However, the author and the publisher do not assume and hereby disclaim any liability to any party for any loss, damage, or disruption caused by errors or omissions, whether such errors or omissions result from negligence, accident, or any other cause.

While every effort has been made to avoid any mistake or omission, this publication is being sold on the condition and understanding that neither the author nor the publishers or printers would be liable in any manner to any person by reason of any mistake or omission in this publication or for any action taken or omitted to be taken or advice rendered or accepted on the basis of this work. For any defect in printing or binding the publishers will be liable only to replace the defective copy by another copy of this work then available.

The book, "Tere Bina: Without you" is dedicated to humanity, and is a salute to the undaunted spirit of life, rising again and again, like a phoenix.

Contents

Foreword ix

Preface xi

Acknowledgements xiii

Prologue xv

1. A True Love Story 1
2. A Journey From The Past, To The Present, And Into The Future 5
3. Stay On Earth 8
4. Why So Much Love? 11
5. Loss Of A Loved One 13
6. The Excruciating Pain 17
7. The Great Despair 20
8. The Big Trauma 23
9. A Fight With The God 26
10. Why Death? 29
11. Has He Really Gone? 31
12. All Is An Illusion 33
13. The Biggest Mistake "i" 35
14. The Only Reality And The Greatest Truth 37
15. The Biggest Acceptance 39
16. What Is Life? 41
17. When I Was A Child? 43
18. The Journey Of Life 45
19. The Grand Design Of Nature And Whole 48

Contents

Existence

20. Walking The Earth	50
21. The Real I And You	52
22. Why Bad Things Happen To Good People?	55
23. Feeling The Vacuum After The Death	58
24. Bouncing Back	60
25. First Meeting With The Spirit	62
26. Seen Standing And He Conveyed A Message	64
27. Feel Me, I Am Here	66
28. Spirit Hugging	68
29. Only Love Is Real And Permanent	70
30. The Spirit World: Our True Home	72
31. We Are Gods	74
32. Divine Calculations And Rebirth	76
33. Creation And Destruction: A Continuous Process	78
34. Caring Hand Of The God	80
35. Memories	82
36. The Biggest Honour	83
37. Unstoppable Emotions	85
38. Unfulfilled Promises, Undone Tasks And Dreams That Couldn't Become True	87
39. Hope	89
40. Living Life Unplugged	91
41. Pains Are Necessary In Life	93

Contents

42. It Is A Mad's World And Every Being Is Mad	95
43. Each Smile Hiding Thousands Tears And Pains	97
44. Met The Spirit	99
45. And, The Show Goes On	101

Foreword

This book, "Tere Bina: Without you" is a life healer. The book presents a real story about a loving family, who lost their loved one unexpectedly and inexplicably, when their life was moving the way, they wished for. The book discusses the journey of life after John. John was son of Smith. Smith's life had changed completely after the arrival of John in his life. There was complete happiness much to the envy of others in Smith's family with John and other members. Smith always accompanied John like a shadow. But one day, John moves on, and leaves Smith and members of family in utter quandary, stranded, distraught and ruined. The book emotionally discusses ups and downs of the life of Smith and members of family after John, their immense pure unconditional love for John, their complaint with the God, fight with the God, sweet indelible memories of John, and finally the tale of bouncing back to life without John. The book is a tribute to the spirit of life. This book is meant for all those who have lost their loved ones. It is a great healer of its time. This book provides a real perspective and true understanding of life. A mere reading of this book will alleviate such a pain got created due to loss of the loved one. While reading this book, reader will experience the healing touch of angels. Coming and going is the design of life.

This book, "Tere Bina: Without you" is an incredible creation, worth reading, a treasure, a very well written book in novel style and yet teaching life and spirituality. The message of God has reached.

- Baba
22 / 03 / 2020

Preface

This book, "Tere Bina: Without you" is another great healer from me. "Tere Bina" is not just a title, but a situation of life, a fact of every being's life. It is not just the story of John and Smith, and members of family, but of every being in this physical world (earth). Tere Bina is based on a true event, only the names have been changed in contents. All contents of this book are true, and are based on true experiences. The reader can recreate or relate this situation to his or her own situation, and then read this book with complete involvement, for his or her maximum healing. The reading of the book will take away his or her pains, instil him or her with happiness, and will develop true understanding of life's volte-face situations and circumstances. Nothing happens for bad. Everything happens for good only. God, the creator, can never do bad of its own creation. Nature is all caring, and our true great mother. How a mother can do something bad? God has designed this existence like this only with ups and downs. Duality exists excluding the God. God is "Advait (non-dual)". There is only one God. It is the only power ruling over the whole creation, which can be sense-perceived, experienced and imagined. Read this book as your own story and experiences. Death is an inevitable fact of life, so is the re-birth after the death. Energy has to manifest itself without any doubt. Science also says so. Birth is manifestation of energy. Energy cannot perish or die. Death happens in every family. The situation, "Tere Bina", "without you" i.e. a loss, should be correctly understood, and then accepted gracefully with no feeling of any revenge or bitterness, and with no sorrows and pains. There are obscure reasons behind every death. Death is an event, which is just right for the deceased, and also, for all those who are really concerned and affected and left back. Every natural death happens at the right time, at right place, and for all the right reasons, no matter what.

Every word of this book, "Tere Bina: Without you" is a tear dried, yet, contains hope, expectations, joy and happiness of life. It is a tribute to the spirit of life.

- **Dr. Yaduvir Singh**
25 / 02 / 2020

Acknowledgements

The resemblance of title of the book, a word, a phrase or contents or styling of this book with actual persons, living or dead or actual events or other contents or things like a movie, a book, a novel etc. is purely coincidental and unintentional. In case, there is an inadvertent resemblance or similarity, author will like to acknowledge all, with gratitude and utmost thankfulness, in anticipation. One may totally disagree with the contents of this book. This book is meant for all those who have lost their loved ones. It is a great healer. This book provides a real perspective and true understanding of life. A mere reading of this book will alleviate such a pain got created due to loss of the loved one. All the visible and invisible powers are thankfully acknowledged.

Prologue

This book, "Tere Bina: Without you" is a healer, a gem, a must read and a worthy collection. It is a rare book. It is not just a book but the extending caring hand of the God. This book discusses life of a family after the loss of their loved one. Family complains to the God about the loss. Family lives in the sweet memories and finally bounces back to life. Reading of this book will take away fear and pain of reader created due to death. Death has been grossly misunderstood by the humanity from the time immemorial. This book nicely describes with explanations the situations arising after the loss of a loved one. This book is a motivation to keep going, and an inspiration. Spirituality has been discussed in a story style. This book is a tool for self-help, and also, for rendering help to the others.

CHAPTER ONE

A True Love Story

Smith descended on physical plane some two and half decades before John followed him, and met him once again in the body form on the physical plane. They had been staying together in the Spirit World, and also, they had completed their many past journey of life in the physical plane together. Earth is physical plane. In physical plane, matter (earth or prithvi, water or jala, fire or tejas, space or akasha, and air or vayu) association with the energy (soul or consciousness) as its component, and is proportionately quite significant. Physical body is gross. Spirit is subtle, which contains soul, and matter elements of space and air. In the Spirit World, energy with least matter component remains. Spirits remain in the Spirit World. The love of Smith and John for each other was too pure, unconditional, intense and overwhelming, at the levels of their body and the soul. Spirits love each other. True love form is the spirit love. It is the love between two energy forms. Spirit is energy. A true identity of a being is its spirit and not the body. In the physical plane, a being is an outcome of sync among body, mind and spirit. In the Spirit World, only mind and spirit remain with a being. Body is shed at the physical plane, which is called as death. The Spirit World is a different dimension than the physical plane. Two beings, which are two bodies and one soul type, are essentially the energies that are quite similar and homogeneous; therefore, these are able to get intermixed easily. It is a story of love between two spirits. John was so desperate to meet Smith in the physical plane and other spirits in the family in the physical plane, that he did not ask for a long time for his this journey of life on the physical plane. John was a soul of higher of level. Rather John asked for a better quality of his stay at the physical plane and not the long life. John preferred "big life" over "long life", which is no doubt a wise choice in the game of life. Before a spirit reincarnates, a spirits meeting takes place in the Spirit World. This spirit meeting is attended by the spirit about to reincarnate on the physical plane, other spirits in the Spirit Group, senior spirits and the spirit guide(s). A Spirit Group is normally a group of some 30 - 40 spirits, who stay together in numerous journey of life in the physical plane, and also in the Spirit World in the afterlife (life after death). Soul mates also remain the Spirit Group. Soul mates are the two very special spirits, which are complementary to each other. In the spirits meeting taking place before birth on the physical plane, in the Spirit World, all the major events like birth, its time and place, family, relatives and friends, physical success, wealth and death are being decided. John took birth in Smith's own family. Smith was his father. When spirits reincarnates in the physical plane, for some initial 3 - 4 years, it remembers everything, and then memory moves from conscious mind to the subconscious mind, and one forgets its spirit connection with other spirit(s) in the physical plane. John and Smith lived their common time on the physical plane in an extraordinary way. Smith always followed John, wherever he went, and also remained with him as his shadow, and took his care to the extent he could, in his full capacity. When John and Smith met each other this time again in the physical plane, they felt a very special connection and the bonding. Smith and John both had highest levels of love and care for each other, which were unexpressed in words but executed through their actions. They were like object and its shadow. This time for this journey of life, shadow (Smith) had awaited arrival of its object (John). Their life went on, in an awesome manner, together for nearly two decades in the physical plane. And then one day, John leaves Smith. John left for the Spirit World. Object had gone, and shadow was left. Smith could not believe it. Smith could not imagine, what happened? Smith wondered for who he really was? John had changed the life of Smith. It was the best time of life for Smith, when he was with John. All was going on extremely well, and then suddenly why this, Smith brooded. Helpless, haggard, distressed and totally distraught shadow (Smith) was left without the object (John), back in the physical plane. It was enigma of life for Smith. Scars and wounds were made on the minds of Smith and remaining members of family. But, John knew, what was good for him, good for Smith, and also good for the family, back in the physical plane. For Smith, it was a situation of a fish without water, and fish cannot die. Without John, Smith war left is despair. John left for the Spirit World for his new assignments of next part of life. Smith and John lived as normal souls, and were oblivion of their destinies. Smith wanted to live with John forever. John and Smith both remember each other every moment. Smith and John's common time on the planet earth was not just two decades, but several thousand years of loving, caring, sacrificing and experiencing each other. Smith found his soul mate in John. Now, John keeps visiting Smith in the physical plane in the spirit from time to time and assists him in his journey of life. Thoughts, energy impressions and vibrations always remain. Memories and past events are relived through thoughts. Love is a permanent emotion, a tendency of mind, and characteristic of soul, which survives physical death. Mind accompanies spirit on to the other side. John helps Smith and the family members, back in the physical plane, from the Spirit World. John peeps at and greets, Smith and family members with every rise of Sun each morning, and sleeps with Smith and the family members at the fall of each night with the rise of moon, all wrapped up in white sheen, glow and radiance of moon, full of tender touches, replete with love and care for each other, as before, as nothing happened, and the life goes on. John smiles with beaming joy to Smith and the family members with each bloom of flower. John touches Smith and the family member with every feel on the body of a drop of water and the blow of wind. John, Smith and the family members eat together without missing their company, any single day or night. It is their true love and its power, true understanding of design of life and faith in the supreme power running this whole existence, which keeps binding all, viz. John, Smith and the family, and always put smiles on their faces. Smith misses John every moment, in his remaining of journey of this life, and wants to cry unstoppably, but is stopped from doing so by John through thoughts (spirit communication between Smith and John). John has truly not gone anywhere.

CHAPTER TWO

A Journey From The Past, To The Present, And Into The Future

Life is a continuous one-way journey, meant to experience, and therefore, must be travelled. Life is not a destination. Life is not any problem to be solved. Life in itself is both problem and the solution. Nature is life. Life is nature. Nature is mother of mothers, all caring and ever protecting. We all present today, have passed many life times before in this existence, may be on this planet, or may be some other, may be in this universe, or may be in some other universe. Spirits remain together in innumerable previous or past life. During their previous life, they give and take. Thus, there is a karmic balance on each other. Karma is the sole reason for every birth. Settlement of karma is the goal of journey of life. Life is a test. Spirits re-join one another in present, and they will once again come together in the future. This is the play of God. Change is the only constant in this existence. Five things, which affect a being, are people, place, time, food and his or her karma. Karma create destiny. Destiny is self-created. John and Smith had travelled from past in the present and will definitely meet in some other relationship in future. Through the lived relationships, not only we learn from each other, but also pay off our karma. The whole existence is a play of matter and energy. Our true identity is spirit or soul inside. We are energies. Energy never dies, thus we are immortals. Karma is being created only in the physical plane. No karma is created in the Spirit World. Spirit World is world of love, sheer joy and bliss. Physical plane is one dimension. Spirit World is another dimension. Spirit World is being's true home. We are only the travellers on this planet earth, and not its inhabitants. John was Smith's co-traveller, as they had travelled some portion of their journey of life together. Life is journey on rough roads. There is not a single being, which did not bear the pains of life. Pain is necessary to feel happy. The whole existence works on duality. A normal being cannot understand the truth of life. It is only after walking through the path of self-realisation and the enlightenment, which gives the understanding of life. True journey is journey within. Smith had understood these secrets of life, so his pain of John leaving him, was alleviated. We all are time and space co-travellers. We travel at different times, and into the different spaces. A let go of the past, is necessary to live the present beautifully. The soul of John knew that some paths of life can never be discovered without getting lost, so he had left Smith. John was not lost, only he was physically separated from Smith, and was always in contact with Smith at the level of spirit. Strength is the power, hidden inside of each of us. Smith had recognised his power. Life is, always keep moving. When stopped, things do not go right. Difficult roads of life always lead to beautiful destinations. It is the reward to a being by the God. It is the journey of life from the past, to the present, and then into the future, which teaches a lot about the destination. Everybody has his / her own journey, and his / her own story. Smith and John also had their own stories with a greater part in common. Smith and John loved each other in true sense. Only love is real and permanent. Life gives the journey and we create the path. Like many times before, life gave journey to both Smith and John, and they created their relationships and destinies i.e. their own paths. A journey without difficulties is no journey. Smith is always thankful to the God for making John the part and the partner of his journey of life. As a matter of fact, there is nothing like past, present and future. It is just expansion of mind on the time reference. We all arrive and depart at the same time. A being must reply every setback of life with an ebullient comeback, which will also make the soul, which has left the physical plane i.e. earth, happy. So did the Smith, and the family. Life should not be taken seriously, but sincerely. Life is a scripted play, directed by the God and enacted by beings.

CHAPTER THREE

Stay On Earth

Smith wondered, whether his experience of John, and the time spent with John on earth a dream? Was it an end of companionship with John? Moments of life should not be missed. It is we, who can make every moment of life, a golden moment. Life must be given a fair chance to live by itself. Spirits descend on earth i.e. the physical plane, in different relationships. John and Smith had a very beautiful stay on this planet together. Life is a celebration. Probably, it was subconsciously known to both, Smith and John. They left no moment of life getting wasted. They, travelled a lot, ate a lot, and enjoyed a lot. Smith hardly had any regret of life, so was the case with John. Smith and John both had given true meanings to their lives. Smith internally knew that John is a much senior and quite advanced soul than him. Smith always admired and venerated John. Smith had always had a feeling of insecurity that John might leave early. Our stay on earth and the journey of life is a test. If all tests, pains, agonies, trials and tribulations, while stay on earth if passed successfully, the God gives one hundred per cent score to the being(s). Our every act during the journey of life must be consciously done, whereas it is really not. Earth is a playground to play, a place to celebrate the life, and a chance to enjoy the true freedom. There is no meaning of success without failure, or happiness without sorrow. There is a continuous play of duality going on in this existence, and the God is player. Since birth is there, so there is death. Similarly, since death is there, so there is a definite rebirth. Birth and death are just transformations of energy. Energy always manifests. We all are energies (soul or spirit), and not the bodies. Any identification of self with the body is a gross misidentification. John and Smith explored their lives, and tried their best to get the experiences of life on the earth (the physical plane). Smith and John both knew that the sojourn on earth is not the end of journey of their lives. The life is forever, life is a continuous journey, and they will again meet each other, as before. Why Smith loved John so much? It is the unconditional pure love, which will create physical re-union of John and Smith one again soon, though both are always connected to each other spiritually, at the level of soul. Smith feels that John could have been his Spirit Guide, as when the life of Smith was set, John left for a greater purpose and cause. The game of life cannot be easily understood. The events and their purposes are too obscure. During the tough times of journey of life, one must completely surrender him or herself to the God. The God helps a being in getting sailed safely on to the safer side, when life is caught in severe storms and the water is choppy. Every being is travelling through time and space in this long and arduous journey of life. The journey of life continues while stay on earth, and on the other side, during the life after death. It is just not a journey for self, but a journey for all those, who have lost their contacts with the Creator of all life forms. Many times a being is born, not just for his or her personal reasons, but for others. These are the beings, who dedicate their complete time of journey of life on earth in helping others selflessly. John descended on earth and stayed here for Smith and other members of family, and not for himself. The Journey of life on earth is a journey of separation and return. The journey of life is a journey towards a much greater experience of one's purposes and the destiny. The journey of life has its sole purpose of experiencing the truth. In each one of us, the God goes along for ride. We are creations of the God, and the creation and the creator are not two different things, but all the same. God lives in each one of us. We all are connected. We all are same. John and Smith are not different but all the same. The sense of separation of beings is due to their ignorance, improper understanding about the life, and a play of Maya, the illusory cosmic element. The whole set of experiences and sense-perceptions of a being, is just a play of mind. Mind thinks. Mind reprimands. Mind creates all experiences of life and the experiences of truths. However, the reality is far beyond all this. Sense of separation is just a fallacy, and a totally false creation of one's mind. One's intellect is a product of this sense of separation. Smith had understood that the life is nothing, but all about management of mind. Mind creates happiness and sorrows. It is the mind of Smith, which sometimes creates delusions of John's separation from him, and also creates the sense of union or re-union. Stay on earth is a part of journey of life. One always has a very clear choice of either getting lost, or to experience a greater purpose and reality of stay on earth. Smith and John, and the family members chose the latter option.

CHAPTER FOUR

Why So Much Love?

Love is an experience of life. Love helps in discovery of life. Loves gives a meaning to the life. Smith and John loved each other intensely. The whole family loved each other overwhelmingly. Love brings enjoyment. Love and tolerance are the bases of whole existence. Smith and the family members always wondered why they all loved John so much. John also loved them equally. Due to this extreme love, Smith always had a subconscious feeling of John, possibly leaving early, but Smith always tried to befool him, and diverted his mind, as there were no apparent reasons for it. This persisting subconscious feeling of Smith about John possibly leaving early accompanied by an unexpressed constant fear, and therefore extreme love between them, was an inkling by the existence, a message by the God, for this sudden big change in journey of life. John came only for spreading joy and happiness, and no other purpose. We all come with different purposes. Some beings come and travel the planet with the purpose of their life as, "to give", whereas, other come "to take", and some, just come "to observe". John came with a purpose of "giving". Love involves unspoken care and considerations, and sacrifices, all selfless and unconditional. Such a love on earth is showered by mother on her children. Mother is an angel sent before the child on the physical plane by the God. Such a love existed between Smith and John, and between the members of family. A true love creates a feeling of fulfilment. A true love is always fulfilling in nature. Love is an expression of the God, expressed by the soul residing inside every being. Waiting is a sign of true love. Smith and members of family are awaiting re-union with John on the physical plane. If love is real, it will never be over, and will always exist. A true love never has an ending. It is eternal and infinite. Such a love makes Smith and family members to always feel the presence of John at every moment of journey of their life. A true love always finds its way. It is the love, when one's feelings do not leave him or her, even if someone leaves. True love heals all the wounds. Love is a divine gift to being, and also a perfect gift to be given. Lucky and blessed are the beings, which love, and loved up. Love gives strength and courage. It is only true intense love, which made Smith and family members to forget that bad moment of life when John had left, feel the John always, understand the life in a much better and broader perspective, exercise resilience, and to hold on. A true love needs not to be perfect, but true. The power of true love is enormous. It is the true love, which makes the God to appear before the devotee, when invoked. Miracles do happen. Nature and existence do not always work on rigid laws, but gives surprises, as per the great design and the orders of the God. Grief is the price paid for love.

CHAPTER FIVE

Loss Of A Loved One

When John left, literally it was an end of the worlds for Smith and the members of family. Smith could not believe, whether John has really left? Has he really gone? Smith always asks these questions to himself, to the nature and to the God. Is it really a loss? When a loved one is gone, a feeling of intense deprivation and emptiness is felt. Loss of John had created a vacuum in the journey of life of Smith and members of family. Grief doesn't go away. As time passes, understanding of life is being developed, design of nature and existence is being understood, and then feelings of sadness, numbness and anger ease out. Smith had understood design of life. Though, it can be a loss for others, it was not a loss for John. Unification and separation, and then again unification, it is how the existence acts. It is a play of nature. Creation, destruction and then again creation, this is the cosmic design. Change is the design of existence. Beings are trapped in the cycle in birth and death. Smith and members of family had well understood this all. Loss and other difficult emotions become less intense, when one accepts these. Situations will be crated in life, changes will occur, but then, beings should not emotionally, mentally and physically collapse, but accept these gracefully and move on. These are the tests of life, and the God does not want any of its children to fail in the test of life. Smith and members of family had passed this very difficult test of life with flying colours. Now, the God has become too caring and too protecting for Smith and members of family than before, as experienced. Physical body of being is condensed form of consciousness. We all are souls and spirits in essence. It is our true identity. Any identification of self with the body is a grossly mistaken identity. Souls of same kind live in a group or a cluster, known as Soul Cluster. These souls of Soul Cluster descend on the physical plane one by one at different times and spaces, meet each other, get into different relationships, pay off their karma, give and take, learn and experience, and then at appropriate take a journey back to the Spirit World. Journey of souls is a very interesting phenomenon. All spirits live in the Spirit World. Spirit World is a different dimension than the physical world (earth). Spirits never die. Thus, a being never dies. We are immortals. At the time of death, spirit leaves the physical body. Some beings see these spirits, leaving the body at the time of death, or spirits present at a place at some moment and then gone away, or spirits movement through the sky. To whom we love, do not go away. They stay with us, communicate with us, eat with us, sleep with us, play with us, celebrate with us, live with us and walk beside us every moment. Angels attend us. It is the design of life by the God. When we are gone from this physical world, we go in the lap of the God. The time that is shared with one, even he or she might have gone now, that time, experiences and memories are never lost. To whom we love truly, deeply, selflessly and unconditionally become an inseparable part of us. True love can never be separated. What can be separated cannot be a true love. Beings live their relationships at the levels of their bodies, which is the reason for sorrow, pain and grief. But if, the relationships are lived at the deeper levels of souls with utmost purity of thoughts and actions, these relationships are really never gone, and become a perennial source of happiness. Thus, it is never a loss of a loved one. Love never creates a feeling of loss, but creates a feeling of gain. In the game of life, as a matter of fact, there is nothing like loss or gain. Life is an experience in itself with no definitions. Smith, John and members of family are always together, the rope of true love binds them together, and there is no feeling of any loss. Smith, John and members of family live their lives in completeness. It is the power of true love, a blessing of the God. It may be difficult today to see beyond the sorrow, but may look back in memory, greatly helps and comforts. Smith and member of family are always thankful and indebted to the God, for having sent John into their lives. The life should not be appraised just by the time spent together, but by quality time spent together, no matter less or more. So was the case with John, Smith and the members of family. They really lived a quality time of their journey of life on earth, with no sense of individuation, but in complete integration with one another, like so that a pinch on one, was first felt by the second, and the third screamed. This sense of integration is never over, as it happens at the level of souls, which are always connected. As a matter of fact, connections at the levels of souls are true and permanent, and rest are just superficial and ephemeral. Smith and members of family live an inspired and spiritual life full of encouragement. Smith and members of family see the proud, smiling, beaming and radiant face of John, always looking at them from the skies of heaven, and showering his love on them as usual. Death is a promotion, and not a demotion or a punishment, in the process of life.

CHAPTER SIX

The Excruciating Pain

John's departure had left Smith and the members of family in an excruciatingly painful state. John was eldest son. Eldest child in the family always has a very special place in the life of father, and the youngest child in the family always has a very special place in the life of mother. Death comes like a big Tsunami, which just devastates affected beings, and considered as the biggest tragedy by the humanity. It is their sheer ignorance, effect of wrong conditioning and knowledge, and a great misunderstanding about the life. Birth and death are two, out of many experiences of life. Both, birth and death are just two changes. Death is not an end, but just another state of life, "the afterlife". Smith and members of family had knew all this, and understood that death is a temporary freedom. The experience of death is a very different experience. Just before the moment of death, the mind of dying being screens the journey of life before the being in fast forward mode. If the journey of life of being was good, it gives a sense of contentment, and if it was bad, being helplessly regrets. A being has to live in the same state of mind till next birth, in which he or she had died. Heaven is the contented and happy state of mind. Hell is the state of mind replete with regret, remorse and compunction. Mind goes with the spirit after the death. Only discriminatory ability of mind is lost after the death, and being has to live with the tendencies of mind on the other side till next birth. During journey of life in the physical plane i.e. earth, discriminatory ability of mind exists, therefore, by discreetly exercising the free will, a being is able to bring its mind from discontented state to contented state. Same heaven or hell even exist during the journey of life of being in the physical plane before death, as sense of heaven or hell are the two states of mind of a being. Mind creates experiences of life. Heaven and Hell are another two experiences of life. Thus, Heaven or Hell exists before death, and after the death. At the moments before the death, hearing is the last sense, out of five senses of being, which is lost. Therefore, what a being hears leaves its maximum impression on mind of a leaving being. Thus, only good, soothing, calming and peaceful words must be spoken before the leaving being. John always saw the brave face of Smith, and members of family, and heard the words of courage, at that big moment. Normally, rebirth happens between 6 months and 3 years for normal beings, however, it may be delayed up to 12 years or even more for bad souls. A delay in next rebirth also happens for extremely good souls as the required conditions for their rebirth are not readily available. These extremely good souls take birth only through extremely good (in religious and spiritual senses) father and mother, and it takes time. These bad souls become ghost or poltergeist or demon after the death of being, and have to live the period up to their next birth, in a highly tormented state i.e. the state of hell. Good beings live their period up to next birth in the state of great enjoyment and happiness i.e. state of heaven. Death for good beings is a very sweet, gratifying and a fulfilling experience, in which there are no pains and only happiness on the other side. Normal and good soul or spirit, after leaving the body of being at the time of death passes through a tunnel or a spiral on to the other side, for taking rest and getting healed. Bad souls are held at the earth i.e. physical plane, after the death due to being's bad and sinful actions, and mind's strong tendencies, unfulfilled desires and strong attachments to the physical things. These bad souls are earth bound, and keep moving in the lower physical plane from one place to another, and scare and trouble beings having weak aura. John is a good soul, and currently taking rest, and getting healed in heaven. Thus, after having learnt all this, "the excruciating pain" of Smith, and members of family, had gone away.

CHAPTER SEVEN

The Great Despair

Smith and the member of family were in great despair after John moved on. They felt cheated by the life, when their physical relationships with John, were snapped like this, so Smith and the members of family, all decided to win this game of life for all i.e. themselves and the John. Their despair was quite deep. It was like an abyss, which had swallowed all their dreams. Their grief for John was vehement. But soon, Smith and members of family realised that the hope and despair lead to the same destination. Hope is a healer. Despair only wears out a being with no positive outcome. They (Smith and members of family) chose to follow the path of "hope". Now, their despair had gone, as hope and despair cannot coexist. It was the hope of meeting John again. It is the play going on in existence, and it is how it works. We are never separated for a long time. Same souls meet again and again in life, it is the design of existence. Same set of souls meet each other in the Spirit World, and in the physical world. One never knows, how much strong he or she is, till being strong becomes the only choice. Speaking truly, life of a being only begins on the other side of despair. Death is an inspiration. Death is a hope, and not despair. As every failure, makes success closer, so is the death. Looking at death gives a true understanding of life. It gives a motivation and inspires beings to live meaningfully, happily, and with love and contentment. Death is a hope of rebirth. Without death, the cosmic attributes (planetary influences, associated energies of time and space) of a being are not changed. To change the present, past must have changed. A rebirth creates opportunities for better fortunes, as per the karmic accumulation of a being. Rebirth is not possible without death. Initial conditions have a major role of the life conditions. Life is a test, and can never be understood without change. Death is a change, and not the end. Birth is another change, and not the beginning. These changes have happened many times before in the life of a being. Life is a kaleidoscope, with continuously changing of its patterns. What was yesterday is not in the present, and what is in the present, will not be there tomorrow. It is the state of despair, in which a being is able to figure out the grace and presence of the God. Pains, miseries, sorrows and despair are the messengers of the God, and must be attended to with respect and full acceptance. The very purpose of journey of life is to correct the follies and mistakes of life. All the powers of universe, always work for better and better of beings. There is nothing like happiness or unhappiness in the journey of life. These are mere false definitions and associations created by the beings, and are the reasons for miseries in their lives. The existence listens very carefully to beings. If a being choses happiness, more and more happiness will come to that being. On the contrary, if a being choses to remain unhappy, more and more unhappiness will come to the being. As a matter of fact, happiness or unhappiness, hope or despair, are not the situations or circumstances or conditions of the being, but the choices of the being. The existence very carefully listens to our thoughts, respects the thoughts, and eventually makes it to happen in the life. The existence exercises its power of "amen", meaning "so be it", and the thought or the choice of being, and becomes a corresponding action or an event in the life of being. Action is an antidote of despair, therefore, a being must act in order to dispel despair. Smith and members of family had fully understood this game of life (hope and despair), and chose to go with hope, thus, all their despair and emptiness had gone, and promised to John at the level of thoughts to live the life as before when John was with them, along with sweet memories of John, and showering their unconditional love on him (John) as always. For Smith and members of family, every sunrise was the rise of hope over despair, created due to physical absence John in the journey of their life.

CHAPTER EIGHT

The Big Trauma

For Smith and members of family, the moving on of John, had created a big trauma. A trauma is a fact of life. It is created due to our emotions. It is created due to wrong understanding of death, eternal nature of relationships in life(s), and the design of life by beings. Trauma is a part of life and necessary for soul evolution. However, trauma should not be made a life sentence. All the events happening in the life, is an outcome of karma, done either in this life or previous life (s). Thought is the first and the biggest karma than the action. Trauma is a distressing emotion, too overwhelming to bear. A true relationship creates love, an unconditional love, and only love is permanent. A true relationship does not create pain, sorrows, trauma or miseries in one's life. If these are created, it is not a true love, and also true relationship. A space is created by all other beings, which come across in one's journey of life. In the physical absence of being, this space must be filled with true love for them. A true relationship is based on complete selflessness. Trauma occurs due to emotional instability of beings. Smith and members of family had good understanding of events and the life, due to their interests in spirituality, therefore, the big trauma created was too short-lived. In essence, we all are thoughts. It is one's thought about the other, which creates recognition and identification. The thought always prevails. The sound may end, as sense-perceived, but the melody lingers on, as experienced. For Smith and members of family, this melody of John was very much present all the time, and there was no trauma. The thought of being prevails, even after the being is physically gone. This whole universe is a thought. Only thought is permanent. Rest is temporary and ephemeral. Physical body goes away one day, but the energy (spirit or soul) always exists. Thought is energy. Love is thought. Love is energy. Time and space are also energies. In this whole universe, either a thing is a matter, or energy. No one ever comes (birth), and also, ever goes (death). All remain here only. Only, there can be some time and space differences about their existence. Death creates a change of worlds. Death is always fair. Life is a lie. Death is a truth. As air, light, sound and fragrance fill the same time and space together, similarly, there are different realms and dimensions of existence in this whole creation. It is the incapability of a being due to which he or she is not able to figure out the beings in their spirit forms. With meditation and certain other yogic practices, a spirit can be easily sense-perceived and interacted. It is the deepest pain in the life, which lets one to grow into his or her highest self. Love sees what is, but trauma obscures. Trauma is veil, remove it, and see the being with the eyes of soul filled with pure, unconditional and abundant love. A soul can always see another soul. Use the third eye. John, Smith and members of family, all are living together, with no space for trauma in their life, but space only for love for each other. Trauma is a black and darkness, whereas, love is a white radiant healing beam of light. Love does not end with dying. The best of the things in this existence are not seen or touched, but only felt. Birth and death are illusions, life is a constant transformation. If life is lived deeply, all fears and traumas are gone. Now, Smith and members of family were living their lives more deeply than ever before.

CHAPTER NINE

A Fight With The God

Smith and members of family fought with the God over John. They asked, "Why you took John away". They considered God to be very harsh and cruel, and even stopped believing in God's existence. They thought, if there would have been a God, John have not been taken away. But they forgot who had sent John in their life? This question and the blame on the God were replete with uncontrolled love and emotions for John, and quite selfish in nature. They even questioned the God, "Why bad things happen to good people"? John in his spirit form healed Smith and members of family. John answered all questions, which Smith and members of family had posed to the God. Soon they realised that moving on of John was for his (John's) good and our good. The anger of Smith and members of family was like the anger of that child, whose best toy is taken away by the parents, for his or her growth and betterment. Initially, child thinks that his or her parents are very cruel, but soon realises the motive behind, and then feels sorry to his parents. They (Smith and members of family) also realised that their blame on the God was uncalled for, they begged to the God to forgive them. The God is all caring. The God is parent of parents. The God looked at them (Smith and members of family), and smiled.

God gives life. God created birth and death. Birth and death are God's decisions. It is the play of the life, directed by the God. If there is no death, there will be no birth. When a being dies, his or her birth is already fixed by the nature. Death is the cause of rebirth. Every breath is God given. The difference between "no death" and "death", is just the missing out a single breath. When we get tired in the journey of life, or there is no cure available for an ailment, the God puts its arms around us, and says "come back to me". Such a decisive ailment or event is given by the God, and a part of life journey's design of that being, based on his or her present and past karma. Therefore, it is very important to love the being, which is being sent into the life, as God will need him back soon. More good is being, more sooner will be his or her move on. God needs good beings. Good beings are sent by the God, only for short time duration to spread peace, love, happiness and joy. They descend with a strong purpose, say to unite the family, or to give a direction to the family, or to being peace and prosperity in the family, or to bring harmony among the members of the family. Often, it has been observed, that a being changes the whole fortune of a family, or becomes a link of sweet ties and stronger relationships between two discordant families. Such good beings do not undergo their miseries of life, as they really do not have any, but take the pains, miseries and ailments of others onto themselves. These good beings come in the journey of life, only to give. So was the John. The God takes away such good beings to the paradise. Death only takes away the body of being. Soul goes to the God. Mind holds the memories, and heart keeps the love. And, faith confirms us that we will meet again. The fight of Smith and members of family with the God, over the John's move on was soon over. They (Smith and members of family) completely surrendered to the God, perform their all actions and duties with great love while always remembering God and John, and living on peacefully with the faith of physically meeting John very soon again.

CHAPTER TEN

Why Death?

Smith and members of family asked the God, "Why death"? The God replied, "Where is death". The God said, now John is with me, more protected and loved than before. There is a much greater purpose of life and assignments to be given to John now, the God said. John has been promoted in the job and process of life. Smith and members of family were convinced. Smith and members of family asked the God, "Can we see and touch the John"? The God said, more than that, go inside, now John is a part of you. Birth creates a false sense of separation, but death is an undoubted union. The God further said, go inside down of yourself through the ladder of love, and you will meet John. And, the Smith and members of family did exactly as the God had said, and found John in each one of them. Death is an inevitable fact of life. It comes later or sooner. The life has been designed like this. Death knocks at every door. Death is giving back to nature, what one had picked, accumulated and gathered from nature over the journey of life. Thus, nature is a perfect lender. Death is a long sleep. It is an opportunity to take rest and get healed. Death is a fiction. It does not exist. Death is a long rest or a sleep, and a respite from sorrows and distresses, pains and miseries, and trials and tribulations of life. Death is for good. Death should be honoured. Death is the graduation day from the college "earth". This existence works on principle of duality. Since birth is there, so there is death. The design of whole creation including the nature, and the life, is like this only. There is union and separation going on continuously in this cosmic play of life and the existence. There is a continuous destruction and construction in this universe. In this whole existence, magic is happening all around, and all the time. The events happening cannot be either understood or explained logically or through science. And, the greatest magician of this magic is the God. Nothing is for real in this existence. Everything in experience is mere a delusion and a fallacy, a game of mind, an effect of Maya the illusory element in the cosmos. Everything is continuously changing. There is nothing like birth or death or any other event. Every happening or event is just a play of matter and energy, or energy. Natural death is a respite from evil effects created by the mind, and a divine blessing. Smith and members of family had understood this great magic of the greatest magician i.e. the God, in the script of life. Now, they were left with no grudges, grievances, regret, remorse and repentance. The God had already given them (Smith and members of family) many signs of presence of John, and also of his physical comeback at an appropriate time best suited for all.

CHAPTER ELEVEN

Has He Really Gone?

Smith and members of family always feel presence of John. They (Smith and members of family) always feel absolute peace of mind. When one is able to narrate a tragedy without a single tear in the eyes, it shows that he or she is completely healed now. We all are accompanied by a spirit guide and many other angels in our journey of life. The spirit guide and the angels remain in the spirit form, and hold us, all through our journey of life. A spirit guide is an entity that remains as a disincarnate spirit and acts as a guide or protector to a living incarnated being. Spirit guide is the mentor of a being. Our true identity is our spirit, and not the body. Spirit never dies. Spirit is energy. Body will be shed one day. Body is matter. Thus, a being is a composition of matter and energy, like every other entity in this existence / creation. Spirit guide, at the level of thoughts, tells every reason behind the event(s) of life, if implored, and also, consoles / heals us. It is the design of the God for its creation. We are children of God. As parents never leave a child, similarly the God, our divine parent never ever leaves us alone in the life. Physical parents have their limitations, but the divine parent, the God is limitless. God is the parent of parents. Surrender the life to the God, and then see the magic in the life. Life is beautiful, truly a celebration, a great experience, if lived with this sense and understanding of full gratitude, total surrender and complete subservience to the God. Nobody goes anywhere. All exist here only. Nobody ever comes and ever goes, as something can never be produced from nothing. It is something, which results in the other thing. Principle of Cause and Effect(s) is the basis of this whole existence / creation. The same principle, just in other words, is the Law of Karma. Our experiences are the proofs of our existence. Experiences are not only physical in nature, but majorly spiritual in the nature. Creation of thought which results in every action done by a being is essentially a spiritual experience. Something that can be measured by the physical means is physical, whereas, something which cannot be measured is spiritual. A thought cannot be measured by the physical means, but identified from the action, when moved backwards. First thought comes and then action is done. John has not gone anywhere. His moving on, was just a major change or transformation in his life. This move on is a divine truth, and will happen to each one of us one day. Smith and members of family, live with John as before, with the only difference of changed experiences.

CHAPTER TWELVE

All Is An Illusion

Only love is real and permanent. Relations, births and deaths, other events of life, all are illusory (not real) and ephemeral. All experiences in this life are illusory and too temporary in nature. No experience is for real. Life itself is the biggest lie and an illusion. World is an illusion. All problems are illusions of mind. Experiences in life are the play of mind under influence of Maya. Nothing is for real in this whole existence. Everything is left back, and the being moves on, for a next come back again. The whole existence is just a play of matter and energy, where all events are happening simultaneously and no event is for real. With birth, death is confirmed. And with death, birth is also confirmed. Miracles do happen. A miracle is a known effect of unknown cause(s). Energy has to manifest, it is its true nature. We all are energies, the Atman, the consciousness, and nothing else. In this illusory world, then why to get serious? All that has gone was actually never ours, and we will get it back once again, rather again and again. It happened in every past life, and will keep happening till eternity. Smith and members of family understand that John was god's child, and had come into their life with some purposes. We all are god's children. We all come with certain purposes. Life is never purposeless. The whole existence is causal in nature. There is a cause for every effect. Cause is the purpose. Event or action is just its effect. Cause is important, and not the effect. Only cause(s) to some extent is / are in the control of beings, effects are not in the control of beings. Effects are created by the God. Every cause and its effect(s) is a lesson of life. Life is a lesson. Life is a test. Take it, and then learn from it. We all live in dreams. Our mind manufactures illusions. We all are mad. Some beings more mad, some beings lesser mad, and that is the only difference. The whole existence is in a constant state of transformation. Good and bad, perfection and imperfection, all is just an illusion. We should not be judgemental. Let life and its experiences be left as they are without concluding anything about it. Conclusions are the reasons of sorrow, miseries and pains. Witness the life, and do not indulge into it. Indulging into the life is the biggest folly. John came to teach all this only to Smith and other members of family. Reality is persisting illusion(s). Unexpected is the reality in life. There is magic happening every moment and everywhere. An enlightened being witnesses and enjoys this magic. He or she admires the magnificence of this magic. An enlightened being adores the existence. Time is an illusion. Space is an illusion. Being a "being" itself is the illusion of life. Smith and members of family had now learnt to draw their life without using eraser. John teaches them (Smith and members of family) from the heaven.

CHAPTER THIRTEEN

The Biggest Mistake "I"

Sense of "I" is biggest mistake and leads to gross misidentification in a being. "I" creates a false and odious personality. "I" is the most selfish one lettered word. It leads to many evils in the life. Sense of "I" creates separation and individuation. Fortunately, Smith, John and members of family never lived with the sense of "I", but lived with the sense of "We". It was a divine blessing on all of them. It was the reason of their happiness earlier, and even today, after moving on of John, makes Smith and members of family to live happily and sail smoothly through the choppy waters of life. "I" means illness. "We" means wellness. Living with the sense of "I", leads to spiritual disaster and complete ruination of a being. In the life of a normal being, most of the things revolve around this sense of "I". Sense of "I" in a being creates expectations in him or her from the others. No single being is born to fulfil the expectations of other being. Sense of "I", which leads to sense of "me" and "mine", is the greatest trouble. In this existence, there is genuinely nothing like I, me or mine. All is of the God and by the God i.e. the supreme energy. It is the collective wisdom and the collective consciousness that runs the life of all in the existence. And, there is life, life and the only life in the existence. There is change and life, change and life and the process of existence goes on like this. "I" has no place in a commune and also in the nature. "I" creates wants in the life. "I" leads to the habit of "taking and collecting", and not the habit of "giving". A great soul, does not ask for anything for him or herself from the God, but does everything for the God in the journey of life. Sense of "I" leads to utter frustration, chaos, bad relationships and ultimately culminates in a miserable life. Every being is born with dignity under the divine influences, grace and blessings, therefore, must complete the journey of life with realistically set and created attributes of life. Doing so, is one's biggest gratitude to the God. Sense of "I" puts a being in manacles and bondage, whereas, the sense of "We" provides true freedom and liberation in life. Smith and members of family live with, having God as the eldest member and complete owner of their family with no sense of "I", and find John with them (Smith and members of family) always.

CHAPTER FOURTEEN

The Only Reality And The Greatest Truth

Death is the only reality, if born. Death is the greatest truth. Smith, John and the members of the family, all knew about it. We all are born with this reality and see it (death) in the society every other day. We all are spirits. We all are energies. Therefore, we all are immortals. Energy never dies only changes its form. The best place of greatest peace, the ultimate rest after death, and of self- realisation is cremation or burial ground (graveyard or cemetery). Death is a part of life. Death is next adventure. If life is not lived with virtues and the highest principles, it is death while living. A life unlived is death. Death is going back home and living with the God. Majority of beings are already dead. True death is not the loss of the body but the death of morality. Fortunately, Smith, John and members of family rarely compromised with their virtues and principles. It was a divine blessing on them (Smith, John and members of family). Probably, they (Smith, John and members of family) all were born with virtues and principles, carry forwarded from previous life. Souls of same kind live together. It is the law of nature, and the bases of how families are created and who comes in our family. Karmic account of a being decides its birth, place and time, family, relatives, friends, surrounding and the nature of journey of life. We all come to pay off our karmic debts on each other. The moment debt is paid off, we leave (move on to the other side) for a new assignment and a new journey of life. Death is not the end of relationships. Life and death are same and not different. Love does not end with the death, rather becomes more intense. Smith and members of family intensely love John. Death is just leaving to meet again somewhere someday. Life is a continuous journey. Death is beautiful. Death is true freedom. In reality, death is an illusion, and so is the life. No experience in life is for real. Good and lovely souls are always loved and never forgotten, like John.

CHAPTER FIFTEEN

The Biggest Acceptance

Accept the death only as an event in the journey of life. There is nothing like death. Death is just an event like any other event in the journey of life. Death never occurs. Death is just a change in life. We all are energies. Energy can never die. Consciousness is the purest energy. One should do good karma in the journey of life. Death cannot erase good deeds done by a being. A meaningful death is several times better than a meaningless life. Accept all the acts of God with humility and respect. Accept all the happenings occurring in the nature. All big events occurring in the journey of life are predestined. Birth and natural death are predestined. Birth, death and life are not distinct but all the same. Nature is replete with gifts and surprises for all beings. Smith, John and the members of family knew about nature's forces and the actions. Death is not the loss. Loss is what dies within us, while we are in the journey of life. A continuous remembrance of person, who has moved on, defies his or her death. We all will be in the same state one day, where we will meet once again. Between living and the dead there is only difference of their states viz. physical and the spiritual, whereas both are existing together at the same time in the same space. Death understanding and acceptance results in freedom and peace of life. Remembering and accepting the death removes the sense of any loss in life, which is always the greatest fear in the journey of one's life. Essentially fear of death is the fear of life. Those beings fear it, which have not lived their life fully. A fulfilled and contented life is always ready to welcome and accept the death. Smith and members of family are always reminded of this event, which impels them (Smith and members of family) to live their live fully.

CHAPTER SIXTEEN

What Is Life?

Life is a trap, a jail. A trap created by one's own karma. It is a trap or a loop of birth-death-birth. This loop is existence. There is no other purpose of life except soul's advancement. Every being had existed here since the time of the whole creation, and will continue to exist till eternity. An advanced soul had control on its birth and death. The final state of soul advancement is dissolution of all karmas leading to final integration with the supreme soul or energy i.e. the God. Smith, John and members of family were aware of all this drama of life. Every being knows everything about this life drama at the level of subconscious. Every journey of life is a test of life. Soul advancement occurs when a being passes these tests, and then there is a change in the species form. Gender is decided just for the purpose of creating different experiences and understanding of the relationships. Every act of nature and the existence has a very strong purpose. No act of the nature is random. It may look random, but in essence it is well organised. No creation is purposeless. When the purpose is over, there is a transformation. Nature exhibits and manifests itself through play of matter and energy. If everything is perfect is life, as a being wishes, then no learning will take place, and also, no soul advancement will take place. Life should be lived with no complaints. The God has given everything to everybody that he or she best deserves. Since no two beings have same karma, therefore, no two beings will ever have same design of journey of life. Thus, there should be no comparison. Only, a proper understanding of life is needed by all beings in order to live it. Life is always unpredictable. Life has its own ways and methods of teaching us. More difficult it is, more beautiful will be its destination. Have faith in the God, respect for the nature, and patience in behaviour, and then see the miracles happening in the life. Life is an experience and nothing else. Our own thoughts, wrong beliefs and understandings are reasons for our troubles in the life. The nature is all caring. The God has created the perfect design for every being for its journey of life. As everything is perfect, then why to get angry, sad and depressed. Depth of life matters, and not the length of life. Every journey of life gives a chance to one to explore and find, and edit and create the self. Identification of true self is quite important. Giving love is the goal of life. What one gives, the same is being returned to him or her. It is the law of nature, and also of the science. It is the karma theory i.e. the law of karma. Though, life is greatly pre-destined, however, it also largely depends upon one's responses to the situations getting created at every moment in the life. Smith and members of family knew that the beings will come and go away in the life, but the right ones, the pure and affectionate souls like John will always stay with them. John is their hero, "the hero of life". Behind every hero, there are so many other heroes, all is God's blessing. Smith, John and members of family are God's loving, beautiful and blessed souls.

CHAPTER SEVENTEEN

When I Was A Child?

So many things, which happened in the family and the surrounding, impacted me when I was a child, and made me what I am today. I had loved some beings with utmost purity, and also received their love for me. I had seen many deaths in the surrounding. Death was the event which jolted and depressed me most. As a child, I could never understand death. It only scared me. Smith shuddered, and was launched into a soliloquy. Smith was born and brought up in an atheist family. So he could not ask the question about death to the God, nor to the other members in the family due to hesitation considering that may their states during such happenings be same as his or even worse. Thus, Smith feared death for a long time in his journey of life, as he had no understanding of life and life dynamics. When John was born, Smith was in seventh heaven, and got inkling that John is a gift of the God, given to him. John's arrival had brought phenomenal positive changes in the life of Smith and members of family. Now there was peace, love and prosperity in Smith's family. Smith had always wondered that all these positive developments that took place in his family after descend of John, cannot be outcomes of his endeavours alone, but largely created by the forces of the universe. John's arrival in Smith's family was a grace of the God. Unconditional love is the essence and the very purpose of life and also of the whole existence. When John moved on, Smith and members of family understood the life and the life dynamics, and were confirmed that the God had sent John with certain purposes. We all come with certain purposes of the journey of life, and the moment these purposes are over, we move on.

CHAPTER EIGHTEEN

The Journey Of Life

The journey of life is a roller-coaster ride. Life is too short, therefore, enjoy the ride. We meet so many people in the journey just because of our karmic connections with them. Every relation viz. mother, father, son, daughter, brother, sister, husband, wife, relatives, friends, neighbours etc. is based on our karmic connections only. What happens to us in due to our karma? Every event of journey of life is outcome of karma done by the being. Past appears as present, and the present will appear as future in the journey of life. Life journey is a melodrama. It is a journey from childhood to the young, and then old. These are the states created by the matter. There is no change in the energy within i.e. the soul. Energy (soul) arrives, associates with the matter (body) and then departs, when matter is not able to hold the energy anymore. Life is a continuous journey. It is a continuum of infinite cycles of birth-death-birth. More a normal being, life is composed of infinite life journeys. Profile of life is based on one's karma past and the present. Smith, John and other members had a clear understanding of the journey of life. Ups and downs are the part of the script of journey of life. Worries do not solve the problems. It is the perspective towards the life, which matters and solves its problems. No problem in the life is really a problem, but it is a different experience. In every journey of life, we are born with no apparent experiences, but definitely all die with loads of experiences. "Experiencing the life" is the purpose of journey of life. Life is a test. Life is an adventure. Lessons are to be learnt during the journey of life. Pleasure and pain, loss and gain, all are the part and very nature of the journey of life. One should travel through his or her journey of life with complete equanimity, faith, surrender, persistence, perseverance and patience. To travel light in the journey of life, one should leave, hatred, anger, greed, desires, expectations and comparison. When comfort ends, true journey of life begins. Take rest during the journey of life, if tired but do not quit it. If we quit it, it will again come back in greater rigour with more seemingly punishments (tougher tests) than this journey of life. The journey of life must be enjoyed. Life is not a race. In the journey of life, one determines his or her destination based on his or her karmas. Many paths appear in the journey of life, some paths may be shorter with lesser pains, whereas other paths may be quite longer with pains, but they all lead to the same destination sooner or later. Tougher is the life, sooner one reaches his or her destination. Problems in the journey of life may be due to one's past and present karma, but at the same time, it is also the design of life by the God for that being as he or she is quite an advanced soul. Therefore, do not stop in the journey of life and start analysing it, but keep travelling. Trust the journey of life, if you fail to understand it. Learn to make an enthusiastic comeback and energetic bounce back in the life, no matter what are the events, situations and the circumstances in the life. Life is unpredictable. Communicate with the God. True communication is not spoken and audible, but happens in silence. Life is not a journey outwards, but in essence a journey within. When one life journey ends, other life journey begins. Make the most out of every journey of life. Smith, John and members of family were blessed souls, and had painted their own skies only with beautiful colours of life.

CHAPTER NINETEEN

The Grand Design Of Nature And Whole Existence

The nature and the whole existence are created by the supreme energy, the God. Smith, John and members of family had a clear understanding of the forces of nature and the existence. Beings come in physical form and leave one day. An enlightened being is quite aware of the creation and the creator. Life is a collection of events of all sorts. The nature wants a being to have every possible experience. The expanse of nature and the existence is infinite. It is ever changing and expanding. Except the supreme energy, nobody knows the boundaries of nature and the existence. Beings place and proportion in the whole existence is negligible. There is no place of "I", as "I" does not exist as per the grand design of nature and whole existence, as created by the God. There is only "We" or "Us", as per the design of nature and the existence. Present has emerged from infinite past and will dissolve into infinite future. Being's only place is in the feet of the God. Thus, a being must live with gratitude, humility, modesty, complete integration, surrender and dissolution. Life is a drama, a script written by the being and approved by the God. Karma writes the script. The God has given complete liberty to write the script as a being feels, but the outcome of every karma (the result), the God has kept with himself. The simple rule of life, nature and the existence is, "As you sow shall you reap". Life is beautiful. Nature is all caring and protecting. The existence defines a being as an entity. A being is a part of it, and not a separate entity. A being, nature and the existence, all are manifestations of energy. Energy manifests itself through matter association in the physical plane. Smith, John and members of family, knew that they are different, but same i.e. another you. Drops of the ocean merge with each other and become all the same, once they are back into the ocean. Individuated consciousness ultimately becomes universal consciousness. As, the consciousness gets pure and pure, it merges with the supreme consciousness i.e. the God. Smith, John and the members of family always lived in full reverence to the nature, the whole existence and the God. The nature, the existence and the God are not separate, but one and the same.

CHAPTER TWENTY

Walking The Earth

Beings are born to walk the earth. We all have own paths on earth in the given journey of life. No two beings have the same path. It is so, because we all come to gain different experiences. We all are born with different set of experiences; therefore, the experiences to be gathered in the present journey of life also get different. In each life, we get into different relationships with each other in order to gain and gather different experiences. Smith, John and members of family had lived so many past lives together in different relationships. The present journey of life provided them, a whole new set of relationships. And, their present karma will decide and become the bases of relationships they will go into, in the future journey of life. John was the angel, who was allowed by the God to walk on the earth in the company of Smith and the members of family. The earth does not belong to beings, but beings belong to the earth. That is why we leave, leaving the earth back here, for a next come back in a new form and character. Earth is beautiful and mysterious and so is the life. It is the life and the earth, which all beings have in common. The changes happening during the walk on earth teach us, and make us to progress. The best way to lead the beings is to walk behind them, and this is what the God does? One is never alone in this walk i.e. the journey of life. This walk will not be over till we do not walk the earth end to end, and it is the life. Smith, John and members of family are co-travellers in this walk on earth, every time. The only difference is, some finish their allotted walk early, as they walk fast, and some finish later, as they walk slow, but they meet again to start a fresh walk. The nature of journey of life also depends on the amount of load or the karmic burden with which one walks the earth.

CHAPTER TWENTY-ONE

The Real I And You

I and you are the spirits. Spirit is our real identity. Spirit is radiant cosmic entity. This body is not our identity, but what is inside this, is the real I and you. Smith, John and members of family were well aware of it. This earth is not our home, but the Spirit World is our true home. The God lives in pure heavens, which is filled with love. Spirit World is a dimension or a plane of high frequency and vibrations. Earth is part of material cosmos, and a physical dimension or plane with lowest frequency and vibrations. There are seven major levels or layers or dimensions or planes or spiritual purification spheres with certain numbers of sub-levels or sub-spheres in each, between the earth and the pure heavens. As frequency and vibrations change, time and space definitions also change. In a plane of higher frequency and vibration, one day is equal to many days of a plane of lower frequency and vibrations. Everyone returns to his or her true home a day. It is just a sojourn on earth by all beings. Earth is a spiritual school. Earth teaches compassion, forgiveness and, unconditional unlimited and all-inclusive love to spirits through various relationships and events during their journey of life in the physical form. Thus, earth provides a spirit with numerous opportunities to undo its karma in a much faster way. Descend or incarnation on earth is a privilege. There is a purpose of soul incarnation on earth. Some souls incarnate on earth to heal other souls, some souls come to observe what is happening around and some souls incarnate to experience and assist other souls. Soul incarnation on earth has karmic reasons, and the soul wants to undo its karma during the journey of its life here on earth. On earth, a soul meets other many souls having different levels of awareness and consciousness, whereas, in the Spirit World, a soul or a spirit is surrounded only by the souls or spirits of similar levels of awareness and consciousness. Thus, in the Spirit World there is no learning and soul advancement. Only for learning and soul advancement, a soul incarnates on the earth. The dates of birth and death are pre-decided by the soul in the Spirit World well ahead of its arrival or descend or incarnation on the earth. Major events of journey of life including the members of prospective family are also pre-decided by the soul in the Spirit World well before its reincarnation on earth. Fear and attachments also become bases for type of reincarnation e.g. a rat becomes cat in its next birth, and a snake becomes mongoose in its next birth. Journey of life on earth is not easy. Growth and comfort do not exist together. One's soul inside and the spirit guide are the instructors, who constantly suggest about right and wrong during the journey of life on earth. Loving self, all and everything is expressing love to the God. Smith, John and members of family are the spirits which remain together in every journey of life. Their karmic debts are largely related to each other. Spirits in the Spirit World also live as groups i.e. families. A spirit is surrounded by like-minded spirits all the time. Karma is the basis of birth, death, nature of journey of life, life and the whole existence. After death, spirit returns to the Spirit

World, but sometimes it can be seen as orb, as it visits its family on earth. Bad souls are not returned to the Spirit World, but are trapped in the lower dimensions closer to the earth or the earth itself, and become ghost. However, souls whether in their physical forms or in their spiritual forms, live and stay together. Law of Karma is essentially Principle of Cause and Effect(s). In science, same Law of Karma is Newton's Third Law i.e. every action has an equal and opposite reaction. We are children of the God. Love is spirit's only characteristic.

CHAPTER TWENTY-TWO

Why Bad Things Happen To Good People?

Smith and members of family wondered, and complained to the God that why such a bad thing has happened to them. John had moved on. Interestingly, every being considers him or her to be good. Karma plays its role, and takes its toll. Being's thoughts and emotions usually do not remain in his or her control, and become the biggest reasons for his or her pains, sorrows and miseries. Naturally occurring events of life have been grossly ill-defined, highly misidentified and largely mistaken by the beings. Whatever naturally happens in the life that could not be controlled despite having put the best efforts, is the will of the God, and is never ever bad. Every pain of life makes a being closer to the God at least by one step. Naturally occurring events are neither good nor bad. Definitions of good and bad are created by the beings as per their likes and dislikes, comforts and discomforts. God is our friend and not the foe. Nature and existence care for us. Beings should have a proper understanding of life phenomenon and life design, and should live with the attitude of gratitude to the nature, existence and the God. Accept the natural events of life, and explore the good behind it. Bad has no place in the whole existence. Existence survives and thrives only on love, and not the hate. Smith, John and members of family gracefully took and accepted the favourable situations of life, and paid their gratitude to the God. And also, Smith and members of family tolerated and accepted the unfavourable event of their lives i.e. move on of John, and remembered the God. There is always a good plan behind every seemingly unfavourable situation in the journey of life, not known to us, but better known to nature and the existence. Life goes on at the will and the mercy of the God. A strong belief in God is necessary for soul's advancement. Present comes from past, which is forgotten. The present unfavourable events of life are outcomes of wrong thoughts, bad words and various misdeeds of the past lives of being. Good and bad is just a fallacy, a play of mind of being created because of duality. Remember the God in good times and bad times of life. God is merciful. Live with a complete surrender to the God. Smith and members of family fully understand that only the God had given them John, and now the God has taken him back, and has some higher and better plan for him. Changing the vision in turn changes the whole being. God's vision is different from being's vision. A being plans the future on the basis of present, whereas, the God plans the present of a being on the basis of his or her past and the future. God is the painter who paints a much bigger and a much beautiful picture for all always with the aim of improving the being's consciousness and thereby, advancing the soul. The God has a systematic plan and pattern, and a nice layout and design, for all the lives. Our point of view does not matter. Situations and the events in the journey of life just occur, and these situations and events are neither good nor bad, but are strictly as per the life's point of view i.e. as per the God's point of view. Every soul at reincarnation (at birth) brings along past samskaras and many past karmic debts to other souls and entities, and when leaves the body (at death), takes along new samskaras and new karmic account of the life just lived. Samskara is mental conformation. Samskara is latent karmic tendency, which shapes being's journey of life. Energy sent, definitely returns. The energy of love exchanged between each other by the Smith, John and members of family, returns to them at every moment of life, and gives them a constant push to keep moving in life with zeal and love filled hearts.

CHAPTER TWENTY-THREE

Feeling The Vacuum After The Death

A deep feeling of emptiness had engulfed Smith and members of family due to John's move on. When father or mother or brother or sister or son or daughter or a close relative or a close friend goes away a vacuum is created. This vacuum brings beings closer to the reality of life. On one hand it creates darkness, emptiness and loneliness inside, but at the same time, it stops bad thoughts. Such a vacuum brings along guilt, remorse, compunction, and selflessness. The death inspires a being to do charity, and also help the helpless. Death leaves a strange impression in the minds of beings. Burial or cremation grounds are the places of spiritual awakening. Here, a being gets free of all tensions, anxieties and worries of life. Shiva is easily experienced on burial or cremation grounds. Spiritual processes begin only after addressing the mortality. Life reveals itself only on the creation or burial grounds for normal beings. Loving beings die, but are never buried or cremated in memories. There can be nothing more beautiful than a natural death. Death does not hurt, life hurts. When caterpillar's world ends, butterfly's world begins. Death cannot kill which never dies viz. love.

Memories comfort till we meet again. Smith, John and members of family are tied to one another with the cords of unconditional selfless love.

CHAPTER TWENTY-FOUR

Bouncing Back

Events, good or bad, will keep happening in the journey of life, but life keeps moving. Stopping is death. Moving is life. Difficulties are the part of life and add flavours to it. Smith and members of family had now full bounced back from the setback of John's move on. Life does not deliver the intended outcomes majority of the times since it has to teach us many things during the journey of life. Failure creates winners. Life is beyond failure and success, loss and gain, penalty and reward, and, miseries and pleasures. Best moments come only after the bad moments in the journey of life. One reaches out to the flowers only after having walked on the thorns. Great things in life never come from comfort zones of life. The time taken and the power with which one bounces back from adversities make his real personality. Winners in the life are the beings whose capacity of resilience increases after each setback. Smith and members of family are winners of life. Adversities in life provide opportunities to reinvent the life. The life is an adventure and needs to be explored all the time. Life is meant to be celebrated. Life is a reward, and not a punishment. The enlightened beings have all this understanding about the life. Our reactions and responses create our karma. How one is treated by others does not create his or her karma, but provides an opportunity to pay off bad karma done in the past, and get light. Smith and members of family do not miss John, but just miss who they thought he was. Always remember in life that the God never burdens the souls beyond what they can bear. Beginning again, again and again, is the true spirit of life. Convert sour and bitter into sweet. Bouncing back is not only the essence of life, but also essence of all other related aspects to it, like relationships. It is the biggest gift to all those loved ones who have moved on from those who are still in their journey of life. Life is found after death as peace is found after the war. Nature is the biggest teacher. Nature clearly shows us that day come after the night. A moment is valued only after it becomes memory. Mind never forgets since it has a memory, therefore, every effort must be made to make it to accept a situation or an event, and then continue. Life is nothing but management of mind. Smith and members of family know that in the life we only part to meet again. Spiritually, Smith, John and the members of family are still living together.

CHAPTER TWENTY-FIVE

First Meeting With The Spirit

It was a bright sunshine afternoon a day, and Smith was working in his office. A white plume appeared before Smith's eyes. At the level of mind through thoughts, a message came to Smith that it is John. Smith felt a divine peace inside and was in a surprise. It was John's spirit. We all are spirits. Spirit is our true identity. This white plume stayed there for some time, and then disappeared all of sudden. Spirits from the Spirit World are allowed to visit their family members, who are still in their physical forms and continuing their journey of life. Such spirit visits are allowed for the purpose of consoling, solacing and healing the loved ones left back in the physical plane. Smith was very happy at this meeting. He expressed his gratitude to the God, and showered lots of love on the John. Almost at the same time at some other place, Smith's mother also saw the spirit of John. She is also deeply connected to the John at the soul level like Smith and members of family. If one is ready, the Spirit World shows many things, which otherwise cannot be sense perceived. The Spirit World sends us message of our loved ones from there, through elaborate and simple signs in our daily life. The Spirit

World is much more beautiful, real and lasting than this world. Sense of separation is one of the biggest illusions. When mind quietens, soul starts speaking, and we get connected to the spirits.

CHAPTER TWENTY-SIX

Seen Standing And He Conveyed A Message

In a seemingly prayer meeting after a sudden accidental death of son of a staff member working in the office of Smith, Smith saw his son standing in front of him. He was seen standing quite vivid yet transparent, like somebody standing behind a net cloth. Smith possesses certain psychic capabilities. His son was known to Smith. Smith saw his son smiling innocently. Smith found him great comforts. Death is a great comfort if one's thoughts, words and deeds were good while he or she was in physical form. His son conveyed a message to Smith tell his father and other family members to stop lamenting and grieving. He conveyed a message that he is happy there. After some time, Smith changed his posture and sitting direction, and then his son also changed his direction, and came in front of Smith again. For almost full time, his son kept standing in front of Smith. While return from the meeting, his son appeared on windscreen of Smith's car and said thank you. For quite some time, up to his chest, he was on the windscreen of Smith's car, and then slowly disappeared. It was his thank you for conveying his message to his father and family members, who were not able to see or feel him.

Spirits from heaven never harm us.

CHAPTER TWENTY-SEVEN

Feel Me, I Am Here

Spirits regularly visit the physical world from the Spirit World to meet, greet, heal and love their loved ones, who are still in the mid of their journey of life. Spirit's presence affects our thoughts and mood. Spirit support brings phenomenal changes in life like growth, development, wealth, prosperity, and other physical world successes. There is a complete turnaround in the life. Smith and members of family also witnessed the same. Many big projects, which could not be completed earlier, got completed with no much conscious efforts, energy and involvement. Many times beings move on with the purpose to assist their family from the Spirit World. In physical form there are many constraints, which are otherwise not present in the spirit form. This assistance may be in the form of medical care and cure, money, job problem solutions, success in the competitive and job related examinations etc.. There has to be counterbalance by the nature and existence for the incurred loss. Loss is compensated with gain by the existence. It is the design of life. Duality in the existence has to prove itself. Death compensates itself with birth. There is sudden progress after death. Spirit communicates to its loved ones at the level of mind that I really care for you. Till I am not born again, I am here, Spirit communicates. Spirit presence is in the form of flickering of the bulb, sudden change in temperature, a strange smell, mood and energy, pet's unusual behaviour, listening a whisper, jitter in radio sound, shadows out of corner of eye, touch, getting sudden goosebumps, stopping of clock at same time again and again, computer and / or other digital devices getting ON or OFF all of sudden, sound and music, seeing butterflies, dreams, telepathic thoughts, dust or mist or development of mould on photos, presence of orbs in photographs, feeling of being watched constantly, misplacement of object, hearing someone calling etc.. Reason is powerless and insignificant in the expression of love. Spirit's love is unconditional. When one's mind is pure, the joy will follow like a shadow. There is after death communication (ADC) from Spirit World to the physical world. Smith and members of family frequently connect with John through memories and communication of thoughts.

CHAPTER TWENTY-EIGHT

Spirit Hugging

Spirit hugs its loved ones, who are still in their physical forms. In the spirits photographs, a father's spirit has been seen hugging its children at home. Spirit of husband has been seen along with the wife attending family functions. Hugging is the most beautiful and truest form of silent communication involving giving and receiving. A hug is worth thousands of unspoken words. It expresses power of love, and communicates that you matter a lot to me. Hugging is exchange of two hearts. Spirit struggles and communicates that I am touching you and why you are not acknowledging me. One should be receptive to feel the spirit hug. We all have some psychic abilities, and just we need to hone up these. Spirit is essence of the God, living inside each one of us till we remain in the physical form. Spirit hug makes the being feel better. Smith and members of family have felt the hugging of John many times. We are spiritual beings having human experiences. Love is the only prevailing truth and everything else is sheer illusion. Hugging has a healing power and eliminates grief. Hug is expression of forgiving and makes one to forget the bitter events or behaviour or experiences. Nature hugs beings in so many ways like sunshine, wind, rain, smell, sound, light etc.. Spirit hugging is a very common and frequently occurring phenomenon taking place only if there is pure love between two beings.

CHAPTER TWENTY-NINE

Only Love Is Real And Permanent

When we are in our physical forms and in the journeys of life, we love beings that are special to us. When a being is gone, even then also, our love for him or her persists, rather it gets too intense. So what has changed? That which is real does not change. That changes, is unreal. Love does not change so it is real. As it exists always, whether being is there or not, so it is permanent also. Similarly, our physical body undergoes changes continuously, therefore, it is also unreal. What is real inside us does not change. Spirit and soul is the reality and true permanent identity of beings. Love of Smith, John and members of family is real and permanent. Love and compassion are nature of beings. Love arises from affection. Beings having true love are soul mates. Smith, John and members of family are soul mates. God's love for us is permanent and constant. God loves us before birth, during the journey of life and also after the death. God's love is forever. Love is a self-enlarging experience. Love gives strength and courage. True love gets strong and stronger with time. Love kindles the hearts and leaves a permanent impression. Love is life. Smith, John and members of family love each other no matter what.

Beings who love each other remain together in each and every journey of life. Such beings with true unconditional love had been together in all previous journeys, are / were together in this journey of life, and will also remain together in all future journeys. Spirits accompaniment with being(s) is always there.

CHAPTER THIRTY

The Spirit World: Our True Home

From where, we come at birth? Where we go at death? It is the Spirit World. Our true identity is the spirit inside each one of us. And, the Spirit World is our true home. Spirit World is a different dimension in this existence, other than this physical dimension i.e. the physical world. Shiva is the lord and the supreme ruler of the Spirit World. A greater part of our spirit still remains in the Spirit World, though we may be in our physical form and in the mid of journey of life in the physical world. At the time of birth spirit separation occurs, and at the time of death, spirit reunion takes place. The Spirit World is a perfect place. There are no sorrows and pains in the Spirit World. There is joy, happiness and bliss in the Spirit World. It is a shining world with ethereal beauty full of healing radiant beams of lights, sounds, colours and fragrances. All beings live there in their spirit forms. Senior, advanced and enlightened spirits, all live there. Our spirit guide (the guardian spirit) and angels, all live in the Spirit World. There is love, and only pure love prevailing and pervading all over in the Spirit World. God is seen and interacted with in the Spirit World. We come to the physical world for gathering experiences of various kinds by taking various tests of life as per our divine design. It is necessary for our soul's advancements. Smith, John and members of family knew that the prettiest smile hides the deepest secrets of life, the prettiest eyes have cried most tears, and the kindest hearts have felt most pains of life. They (Smith, John and members of family) know much about the Spirit World, and stay in constant connection with it.

CHAPTER THIRTY-ONE

We Are Gods

God is understood as the creator, the sustainer, the destroyer and the re-creator. For microbes and microorganisms like germs, bacteria, viruses and fungi getting created, living and then propagating themselves inside us, our body acts as their complete world and the whole set of their life experiences. For these microbes and microorganisms, we are gods, as they grow, live and then die inside us. Creator and creation are not too distinct entities but one and the same. Creation carries all characteristics of the creator. Our soul and spirit is an element of God staying inside each one of us. Thus, this physical body is a temple. Temple and the statue inside it cannot be viewed separately, but both viz. statute and the temple are one and the same. Smith, John and members of family knew that we all are the elements of God, and we all carry divine characteristics and properties. An ordinary becomes extraordinary by virtue of its quality of thoughts, words and deeds. Super and advanced souls are quite close to the God, and possess much of godly traits and characteristics. Nature and the existence bow down before such super and advanced souls. These great souls perform acts, which look like miracles to the ordinary beings. Nature and the existence follow their orders. Smith, John and members of family understood that the very purpose of every journey of life is self-improvement and soul advancement.

CHAPTER THIRTY-TWO

Divine Calculations And Rebirth

In this nature and the existence, all events are causal, and not random. Universe looks chaotic, but not, rather it is well organised and ideal. There is always a strong reason and a convincing logic behind every happening. Birth, death and then rebirth all happen as per divine calculations. Death is decided before birth. And similarly, rebirth is decided before death. This existence is a play of matter and energy. We all are energies in essence. Energy is prevailing and pervading all over in this existence. Energy is non-physical in nature, whereas, matter is physical in nature. Our every thought, word and deed, is karma, and creates impressions in our individual and collective energy landscapes. It is called as, "Akashic Record". When somebody dies somewhere, somewhere somebody is born. Joy and sorrow happen together. Duality exists in this existence except the God, the one supreme energy, which is non-dual (*Advait*). We all come from the Spirit World and become part of a family as per certain divine calculations, based on the God's will and akashic records. Akashic record contains all karmic information of a being. Our soul residing inside us, is the element of the God in us, and acts as a judge, and pronounces its judgement for each created karma. This judgement is then endorsed in cosmic document i.e. akashic record in the form of energy impressions. These divine calculations decide the type of species, time and space of our birth and rebirth after death. Smith, John and members of family are conscientious beings, and act consciously and quite scrupulously using their full conscience so as to create a very high quality akashic records. Divine calculations are outcomes of energy interactions, and are based on law of equilibrium of energy. These divine calculations are done continuously, and affect the life and the journey of life of beings. A spirit decides its time and type of death in the Spirit World and inside the womb of prospective mother, well before its descend on the physical plane i.e. birth. Time and space, both are energies. Time energy and the space energy continuously affect our journey of life. These two energies work in sync. The effects of time and space energies for every being are different owing to the difference in their individual energies. Consciousness is memory-less intelligence, and in essence pure energy. Our journey of life is affected by our individual consciousness, and the collective consciousness of the family, neighbourhood, society, state, nation and the world, prevailing at a given time. Also, there are effects of space energy in simultaneity.

CHAPTER THIRTY-THREE

Creation And Destruction: A Continuous Process

Thisexistence is bound by the principle of duality. Since birth is there, death is there. Since day is there, night is there. Similarly, for every creation there is a continuous change in it, eventually leading to its destruction. In nature, all the events are happening at the same time. Creation and destruction is happening continuously, and also, simultaneously. It is a continuous process. What is created today will be destroyed tomorrow. Delay or the sense of time period between construction and destruction is just a play and a delusion created by mind. Mind also contains memory. Memory cannot be understood by the normal beings without creation a time scale or a time reference, though this creation is false. In actuality, there is nothing like time. Time taken between sense and perception creates a time horizon in every being. Time taken between sense and perception is an effect created by the intellect. No two beings have same levels of understandings for time (past, present and future), and also, for anything in this nature and existence. Every being has its own world, even in the given species. One's world is his or her set of life experiences. No two beings in this creation have the same sets of their life experiences. We are individuated consciousness, separated from the supreme and only one consciousness i.e. the God. Smith, John and members of family have witnessed this continuous process of creation and destruction at every moment of their journeys of life, and life, within the family, and also, in the environment outside. Creation and destruction is the nature of energy. Energy manifests itself through its matter association. Both matter and energy have inherent nature of change (mistaken as decay), therefore, in this process of change, events occur, which perchance also happen to be contrary to each other e.g. birth and death, success and failure, joy and sorrow etc., which creates notion of duality. How creation will happen, if there is no destruction? Same thing which is being destroyed is created anew again i.e. re-created. Metamorphoses are the bases of functioning of this nature and this existence. No birth is possible without a death. No event is bad, rather all kinds of natural events are necessary for this existence to exist. It is the will of the God.

CHAPTER THIRTY-FOUR

Caring Hand Of The God

We are never alone in the journey of life. The whole journey of life is under constant supervision of the God. There are many spirits, angels and the spirit guide (guardian spirit) for each one of us, which accompany us, all through our given this journey of life, and the life. It is an arrangement by the God for all of its creation. There is always a caring hand of the God with every being. Every being is supported by the God with one palm above, and another palm below. When John moved on, Smith and members of family were completely shattered and broken. It was the strongest storm in their life. They felt excruciating pain because of this event, and were totally ruined. John's move on had left deep scars on the hearts of Smith and members of family. For Smith and member of family, it was their end as well. They could never imagine without John. But the God has its own plan, not known to us. We plan our future based on present, but the God plans our present on the bases of our past and future. Beings overcome pains, miseries, trials and tribulations of their lives, how big they might be, as there are always forces of nature accompanying and assisting them, and healing and protecting them continuously. It is a readjustment and regulation mechanism in the journey of life by the existence under the will of the God. Purpose of life is to teach various lessons of life. It is necessary for soul's progress and advancement. Bouncing back is the nature of spirit. We all are spirits. There is spirits accompaniment with every being always. These spirits, angels and the spirit guide (guardian spirit), along with the spirit of the being, who has moved on, spiritually communicate us the reason behind this move on, and try to convince, console, comfort and heal us. The caring hand of the God protects us. God's grace increases at such moments. God's love for us gets more intense at such moments of life, as God is the ultimate parent. The God is parent of parents. Our mother and father are our biological parents, but the God is divine parent of all. It is the power of true and unconditional love for John, which made Smith and members of family to keep going joyfully in their remaining journey of life *without you* (John) viz. *Tere Bina.*

CHAPTER THIRTY-FIVE

Memories

Memories are the doses for life with healing capability. Memories are quite vital to life, and play a very important role in the drama of life. Being's memories are the impressions created on quicksands on the shore of ocean of life by feet of being, while walking during his or her journey of life. Physical mind works predominantly on the basis of memory. Only memories are left, when one is gone. Living memories are timeless treasures. Memories remain in mind. Lingering memories remind us constantly about what matters most to us. Smith and members of family constantly live with the memories of John. Moments of life are valued once they become memory. Memories are feelings. Memories facilitate time travel in the past, and make one to find him or herself in the company of his or her loved one once again, who has now moved on. Memories make one to relive the best days of life. A quality life is a collection of happy and good memories of unforgettable moments of life. Memory is scribe of soul, cherish it. Memories make one to hold the things which he or she loves. Smith and members of family are holding John through his memories.

CHAPTER THIRTY-SIX

The Biggest Honour

Being father or mother of a child is the biggest honour bestowed on a being in his or her given journey of life. Not every being gets this chance and honour. It is the grace of the God, and the result of one's past and present karma. Smith and members of family are completely beholden to the God with full gratitude and complete servility, for having sent John in their life. John's arrival completely changed the course of their life. With John, life of Smith and members of family was filled with joy and celebration. John was the best gift of life for Smith. Birth of John was the biggest honour bestowed on Smith by the existence. John is Smith's soul mate, and an alter ego. John is now present in the spirit form. We all are spirits. Arrival of John was the biggest addition in the psyche of Smith, and his move on is the biggest subtraction. All naturally occurring events of life are will of the God, and happen exactly as per the divine design for being. Therefore, events in the journey of life should be accepted with humility. It is so, because still whatever is left, is the grace of God, and more than one truly deserved. Nature compensates loss. Nature has its own plan, not known to us. An arrival is possible only when there is a departure. Life should never be taken seriously, but be always taken sincerely. All the pains and anguishes go off the chest, once there is full dedication and faith in the God. Patience is the key to a happy journey of life. What has gone today, will definitely come tomorrow. Being a being, and being present on the planet, itself is the immense grace of the God, and the biggest honour. All the stages of life are necessary for a complete life. Being old is not a curse but an honour and a reward of life. Journey of life is, being strong and loyal, feeling honoured and accepting the death. God has created life, and is the source of honour and wealth. Life itself is an honour, the biggest honour.

CHAPTER THIRTY-SEVEN

Unstoppable Emotions

When a loved one moves on, remaining members of family are totally upset, completely broken and filled with unstoppable emotions of regret, hate, anger, jealousy and guilt. Emptiness is created in the life of those, who are left behind. Move on of loved one creates a vacuum in the life. It seems that all has gone, and now, there is no purpose left for life. Smith and members of family also cried unstoppably when John moved on. Their life seemed to have come to an end. But nature has its own plan. Slowly and imperceptibly life turns. There is refilling of courage and strength. Healing occurs subtly and gradually. Spirits are most active at such moments. God's grace is too intense at such moments and period of the journey of life. Bouncing back is spirit's nature. We all are spirits. Definition of life changes after such incidents. There is a complete volte-face, and change in the perspective of life, thereafter. But, the life takes its own shape and follows its own course. Relationships are being re-defined. Many truths of relationships and other aspects of life also come to the fore. Connections at the soul level only work and are left, and the rests are gone. Life maintains and regains its pace, may not be same as the original, but in no way inferior to before. Life's design must be understood by beings. It should also be understood that we are not here for always. The loved one is waiting in the heavens, and once again re-union will take place at an appropriate time. Therefore, enjoy and celebrate the life unstoppably, no matter what. Smith and members of family are living their life unplugged, and happily continuing with the remaining journey of their life.

CHAPTER THIRTY-EIGHT

Unfulfilled Promises, Undone Tasks And Dreams That Couldn't Become True

As John had moved on, some of the promises which Smith, John and members of family had made together could not be fulfilled. They (Smith, John and members of family) had together decided many tasks to be done, and many actions to be executed, but some tasks could not be done, and some actions not executed. There were many dreams, which they (Smith, John and members of family) had seen together, but many of the dreams could not become true. Indeed, there was a larger portion of life that was left incomplete and unfulfilled. To complete it, John's rebirth and re-arrival in physical form is inevitable. We all take birth to fulfil our made promises, do the remaining tasks execute the remaining actions, and make the left dreams become true, all carry forwarded from previous births or journey of life to the present journey of life, and also to the future journey of life. There are many places or foreign visits, which are left to be visited, but the being moves on. There are many things to eat and enjoy, but the being moves on. Houses, mansions, luxury cars etc., are left to be purchased, but the being moves on. Rides of snowscoot and jet ski are left, but the being moves on. Parents dream of marriages of their children, and also playing with their grandchildren. Unfulfilled desires and tendencies decide the nature of next rebirth and its associated situations like type and time of rebirth, place of rebirth, future family, relationships, surroundings etc.. Child, who has moved on, returns as grandchild in future. Parents return as children or grandchildren. Life has to experience every relationship. It is the reason why, we come at different times, and also go at different times.

Smith had dreamt about John, doing a decent white-collar corporate job after graduating from a well-known university, living a high quality very rich life thereafter, getting married to a beautiful girl on a lonely and lovely island (a paradise), and playing with grandchildren sired by the John. What we think, we become. Nature listens to our each and every thought. "Law of Attraction" works. There may be an apparent or a seeming delay about the execution of events on the part of nature, but there is never a denial of the execution of events by the nature. Smith, till today, holds all these dreams about John, though John has moved on, and Smith will keep holding these dreams in future also, all throughout his this journey of life. Smith is confirmed that nature will make all these dreams of him about the John, come true one day. Smith is left with no remorse or regret and the grudges. Smith's scars and wounds created due to the John's move on are seemingly healed.

CHAPTER THIRTY-NINE

Hope

Hope is the basis of life. Hope brings motivation. When all is gone, only hope is left. Hope is characteristic of mind. Hope is a divine provision, granted to beings by the God to come out of difficulties of life. Hope is power in itself. Hope is a healer. Smith and members of family are living their life happily with a strong hope of meeting John again. It is a hope of their reunion. Hope is flame of the candle of life. Nature and existence respect our hopes, and make it a reality one day. Faith and patience are the two key elements for success in life. Hope is the music of grief. Every day of Smith and members of family starts with the hope to meet John, and also, ends with same hope. Hope keeps one alive. For success in life, one needs to work hard and the live the life with determination. Challenges are the part of life and life's divine design. There is nothing like failure, as each failure is actually a lesson. There are only achievements in life, and no failures. There is no fall in the life, but only rise and rise. Failure and fall occur due to loss of hope. Hopelessness brings failures in life. Despondence is one's biggest enemy. One should learn from nature. In nature and the existence, there is nothing like failure and fall, but only struggle, achieve and rise. Events in the life are only meant to teach, and make one to rise to the occasion in a more superior way. Kicks by nature are necessary for beings for giving a kick to his or her life. Life is a game, play it well. Smith and members of family have understood this game of life. Zero hope is pain, sorrow and failure. Some hope is the reason of smile, and leads to life's success. Hope makes one to conquer the unconquerable. Life is a battle. The God is all caring and loving. Nature and the existence can never be rude to any being, as it just makes one to become fit to live the life meaningfully with grace and elegance. Our wrong life learning and conditioning are the reasons for our sorrow, pains, miseries and failures. Every event is necessary in life, and is meant for life's good. One should learn to get up after every fall in the journey of life. If one does not get up after a fall in life, one cannot face and confront that situation in life, and failing to do so, one will be completely crushed under the situation, and will eventually get finished. Spirits help us to get up and rise. Whenever caught in such a situation, look up at the heavens, and pray. Help comes in magical ways, might be subtle or gross. Give your best, and leave the rest. Miracles happen. It is the hope that makes one to see and get benefitted from the miracles happening in the life. Hope brings success. Smith and members of family see the light in the darkness. They dream and imagine John. Hope is a waking dream. Hope is holding on till the pain ends. Tomorrow is a hope. Future is also a hope only. Hope is characteristic of the soul. Hope is stronger than any fear.

CHAPTER FORTY

Living Life Unplugged

Life is a celebration, live it unplugged and blissfully. Live the life in full exuberance. Life needs to be loosened up. Being happy is the very purpose of one's life. No being wants to be sad. Joyfulness and enthusiasm are the measures of quality of life. Smith and members of family are living zestfully in complete joy. It is the joy of having been physically with John in the past, being with spirit of John in present, and the joy of being with John physically again. Joy is the ambience of their lives. Well-being is the state of a being, feeling well. Unshakeable belief and faith, unconditional love and remembering the God are necessary for wellness of beings. One can be physically ill, but still well. Wellness is the state of mind. Mind is the seat of thoughts and wisdom. There is great spirits influence on one's mind always, thus affecting his or her thoughts. Thought is the primal and seminal cause of everything in life. In the state of joyfulness and wellness, life energies are too strong. Smith and members of family are able to maintain their happiness. One should do life's audit. Joy and ebullience in life come by giving. What we give, returns to us. There is no reason to be serious in life. No event in the life is bad, no matter what. Death adds value to the life. Death is the biggest gift of life. Karma means making. Life is based on karma. Therefore, one's life is one's making. What one makes, can also be changed by him or her. One should not attach him or herself to something what he or she is not. One's true self, and its realisation, are the keys to live the life unplugged in state of bliss. Love everything, and everything will love you in return. Love is the basis of whole existence. Smith and members of family love John, and John also loves them. Life never ends. It is for ever. They (Smith, John and members of family) are living their lives unplugged.

CHAPTER FORTY-ONE

Pains Are Necessary In Life

Pains are the part of life's design. Pains are the way of paying off one's negative or bad karma. Karma has to be paid off. It is the purpose of birth, and then, journey of life. If there is no karma left, there will be no pain, and also, no birth. It is the state when a being gets free of loop or trap of birth and death, known as Nirvana or Salvation. Nirvana is a transcendent state. In Nirvana, there is no suffering and desire, nor sense of self. Being is released from the effects of karma, and also, the cycle of death and rebirth. It is the final goal of life. Salvation is deliverance of soul from sin and its consequences. The field of academic study of salvation is known as, "Soteriology". Smith, John and members of family understand the importance and purposes of pains in life. Pains are necessary in life, in order to enjoy the life, and give a meaning to it. One's karma is responsible for one's pains. There is a continuous play of duality everywhere in this nature and existence. Sense-perception is only possible because of duality. Duality is the creation of mind. Black colour can only be identified, when there is a reference of white colour in the mind. As failure is necessary to enjoy the success, similarly pain is necessary in the life for being happy in the life. All *Jiva* undergo pains in life. *Jiva* is a living being, or any other entity in the nature and the existence imbued with a life force. An enlightened being neither gets sad nor becomes happy. He or she only witnesses the whole play of existence and the creation, and appreciates it, as no event is true, and he or she has real understanding of the life and life's design. Pains are necessary for soul's evolution and advancement. Smith and members of family are living with the pain of John's move on, and thus, a big negative karma has been paid off, one of the toughest tests of life has been passed. Pains hurt a being, and also change him or her for ever. Today's pain is tomorrow's strength. Time teaches one to live with the pain(s) of life. Happiness does not teach anything. Pain is the teacher of life. Smith and members of family have learnt to smile through their pains. Pains cannot be avoided, but can only be understood, in order to live a meaningful and complete life. Pains are necessary in life. Have full faith and belief in the acts of nature and existence for their effects on life, patiently watch and witness the whole show of life (the life drama), and accept all gracefully with no doubts and questions, in the state of complete surrender to the God.

CHAPTER FORTY-TWO

It Is A Mad's World And Every Being is Mad

Only a mad can struggle all through the journey of life, only to lose everything at the death. With every cycle of birth and death, one comes back to the same state, from where one had started. In the journey of life, happiness is less in comparison to the pains, as the purpose of life is to teach, and it is the pain which teaches. Happiness does not teach. One always worries, and amasses great wealth for its progeny by all means, despite the knowledge of fact that we all are individuals, and are solely responsible for the acts done. No relationship is a relationship, but a dependency. No other normal being can take the pains and troubles of other being on him or her. Smith, John and members of family know it that is why; they do not take life seriously, but only sincerely. Smith and members of family live like mad. A mad enjoys the moment and lives in it without caring for anything, free of all pains and troubles. One should immerse him or herself completely in the present moment only. The quality of this moment lived, affects future moments. True self is discovered and identified only after travelling through the madness. We all are mad with differences in the degree of madness. Spirit loves freedom. Freedom is the essence of life. A mad lives in complete freedom. Let the life to soar high and high, and do not restrict it in anyway, no matter what. The state of zero constraint is the state of complete madness. A mad lives under greater protection and care of the spirits from the Spirit World, as he or she does not care and fend for him or herself. Only a mad can sense-perceive much beyond what is normal. A mad communicates all the time with the spirits in the Spirit World. Madness takes one to extreme and excellence in a given direction. God is seen and interacted, only when a devotee gets mad for God. Extreme love is madness. It is a mad's world, and every being is mad. Being mad, is sanity in mad's world.

CHAPTER FORTY-THREE

Each Smile Hiding Thousands Tears And Pains

Each smile of Smith and members of family, after moving on of John, was hiding their thousands tears and pains. When John had moved on, Smith and members of family were reeling under excruciating pain. Their hearts were bleeding. It was the moment of life, when they felt most helpless and lonely on this planet. John's move on had left deep scars on their (Smith and members of family) hearts, and left them (Smith and members of family) in middle of ocean of tears. Initially, all (Smith and members of family) displayed a fake bravado, as if they are very stable, gave courage to each other, counselled another, however, at times, all broke down without exception, cried bitterly and vented their anguishes and emotional pains for John. They complained to the God, and even held the God responsible for it. Later they realised that it was their mistake and God does everything for one's betterment only. Life's design is like this. It is a story of every being, every family without exception. These events inevitably happen in life. Even the gods, those who had incarnated, had to go through even much severe pains and agonies, and were not spared. Their (gods) pains were a very clear and loud message to the humanity, about how they (gods) responded to such events, and what they had learnt. These were lessons to the humanity through demonstrations. Such events like death never baffled the gods, as they knew the real truths of life. If the design of life and existence is properly understood, a being becomes mentally and emotionally stable, and such events like death do not disturb him or her anymore. A prettiest smile hides thousand pains. We are actors of the drama of life. Our smile or tear, nothing is for real. In reality, there is no reason to smile, or shed tears, but being witness to what is happening beyond control, is the only left option. Big events in life are beyond control, Smith and members of family had now understood it. Smile is the prettiest thing, one can wear. Smile is free therapy. When life gives the reasons to cry, show the life, reasons to smile also. Smile then shows miracles in one's life. Use tears as prayers, as they directly travel to the God, when one is unable to speak. Tears express highest emotions, and are the most efficient way of communication mixed with unspoken words and unexpressed feelings. Smile and tear are the emotions, absolutely necessary for life.

CHAPTER FORTY-FOUR

Met The Spirit

Smith met the spirit of John. Other members of family also met the spirit of John at the same time at another place. When one moves on, spirit leaves his or her physical or gross body. Spirit is dominantly energy, containing the consciousness. Spirit in subtle body form can be easily sighted by those who are deeply and spiritually connected to one another. All physical world relationships may not be spiritually intense. Spiritual connection is the connection occurring at the soul level. Soul is pure energy i.e. consciousness. With the passage of time, subtle body also loses its form, and becomes spherical known as the orb. Subtle body has same shape as that of the being that has moved on, except the size, which is nearly two inches. Digital cameras have ability to photograph spirits. Often spirits have been photographed and seen as hugging or cuddling the members of family, who are still continuing their journey of life in their physical forms. On big occasions, festival and celebrations, these spirits visit the venue and influence the minds of their family members through thoughts. When we think of them, they are present. It is the reason why, during these moments of joy and happiness, beings remember those loved ones, who have moved on. These spirits are spirit guests on the occasion(s) like other invited physical guests. A spirit has sense-perception, knowledge, memory and intelligence. As a matter of fact, when one is in its journey of life, sense-perception, knowledge, memory and intelligence is of the spirit only, and not due to the organ or the concerned body part. A loss of all these spirit's sense-perception capabilities is known as death, whereas all organs, eyes, ears, nose, skin and tongue are still there in the body, then why body is not functioning. Kirlian photography is a photographic technique used to capture the spirits. Kirlian photography is based on the phenomenon of electrical coronal discharges. Smith and members of family pray and wish to meet John's spirit again and again. Spirits reside in the Spirit World, which is another plane or dimension. The Spirit World has its own laws. A spirit is allowed to visit its members of family in the physical plane or dimension, only when allowed by the senior spirits, the spirit guide and the master spirit, ruling the Spirit World.

CHAPTER FORTY-FIVE

And, The Show Goes On

The show of life will go on, no matter what. Show of life is unstoppable. Generations will come and go in future also. We all come into the relationships in each journey of life with a new script. Events will happen, good or bad. Joy and sorrow will also come. One needs to work on mind. Life is all about mind management. The life of Smith and members of family is once again back to the normal, but scars on the hearts are remaining. They (Smith and members of family) love John inordinately, and will continue loving him. Nobody can take their (Smith and members of family) love for John away. Only love is real and permanent. Love is the basis of this whole existence. Doing worry is an idle time job. If one is busy, where is the time to worry? The show run by great show master i.e. the God does not stop ever, whatever may be the situations and circumstances? There are lessons, and only lessons to be learnt, in the given life. If no lesson has to be learnt, there will be no life either, which will never happen. We all are energies. The God is supreme and purest energy. Energy has to exist. As per science, energy can neither be created nor destroyed. Energy manifests itself, and changes its nature and form continuously, therefore, birth and death occur. The universe is continuously expanding. Changes are happening continuously in the existence. Creation and destruction are happening in a cyclical manner simultaneously. It is the characteristic of energy and matter. There are innumerable beings and other entities like Smith, John and members of family in this existence. Smith and members of family are here today in their physical forms, but tomorrow, their forms will also change as per their life's design. Accept the changes, live joyfully and happily, with pure unconditional love. And, the show goes on...

www.ingramcontent.com/pod-product-compliance
Lightning Source LLC
LaVergne TN
LVHW091600060526
838200LV00036B/920